For Barry Lopez,
who wrote back . . .

FIGURE
IN A
LANDSCAPE

poetry by
Diane Lee Moomey

Day'sEye Press and Studios
PO Box 628
El Granada, CA 94018

info@dayseyepressandstudios.com
www.dayseyepressandstudios.com

ISBN: 978-0-9619714-6-5

Printed in the United States of America

Cover art copyright 2015 by Diane Lee Moomey

Contents

To The Reader

Each of the poems in this collection, spanning about ten years, arose from the experience of living in a particular place and, I hope, conveys some sense of the region itself. The sections "Suburbs, Chapparal" and "Flukes" refer to my current life in coastal California south of San Francisco with its shoreline, its whales and wild places, its suburban gardens.

"The Lake Effect" (referring to a weather pattern prevalent around the Great Lakes) comes from a time of living in a farmhouse just north of Toronto near Lake Ontario, and from a brief time of attempted homesteading in the province of Quebec.

"Tornado Warning", "Jacks, a Game" and "Wind" refer to early years in southern Michigan and my first experience with the wildness of weather. "Outbound" and the poems from "Queen Anne's Lace" to "Memorial Day" are centered around childhood summers with grandparents in the Saint Lawrence Valley of upstate New York. "Nadir" marks the time of my familiy's moving back there in my high school years, for mysterious reasons. One of our darkest hours . . .

The poems that remain: love and death, nature, the *ars poetica* and the flights of fancy, belong to all my places.

Some of the poems refer to regional phenomena. I've included notes below, based on questions I've been asked after a reading.

"Ode" *(page 7)* "The Dish" is the local nickname for the radio telescope on the campus of Stanford University, visible from the highway.

"Double DeClutch" *(page 19)* my husband and I once owned an old Land Rover with no synchromesh in the gearbox. Driving such a vehicle requires fancy footwork and co-ordination, and means one spends a lot of time in neutral. In this poem, he's teaching me to drive it.

"Mud into Stone" *(page 25)* refers to the time I maintained a pottery studio, first building and learning to fire my own rather unruly large gas kiln. This one took a day and a half to fire and three to cool down. Unlike electric kilns which have been tightly jacketed in stainless steel for indoor use, the chimneyed catenary arch kiln is is often loosely stacked and for safety reasons requires lots of space, preferably a hut of its own far from flammables .

"Distal Points" *(page 47)* In Chinese medicine, here expressed through acupuncture, it is considered that the stimulation of specific points on the body can affect distant points.

"Tornado Warning" *(page 50)* in the Plains states, where tornadoes are common, a tornado "watch" means the conditions are right for tornadoes to form; "warning" means funnel clouds or the mammiform clouds that produce them have already formed and are moving, endangering the communities in their path. Since tornadoes tend to move in a northeasterly direction, the best place to take refuge is in the southwest corner of a basement. In this poem, since the seven-year-old "I" doesn't have a clue what's coming, only the adults' fear gets me moving. As a display, the sky was quite fascinating!

"Jacks, a Game" *(page 52)* refers to a game played with neighborhood girls, using a small rubber ball and ten six-pointed, three dimensional metal "stars". The jacks are tossed and scooped while bouncing the ball, each level of the game requiring more dexterity; the fanciful names in italics refer to each level.

"Young Man in Winter" *(page 72)* in places where the ground freezes hard, funeral processions watch the coffin being placed in a mausoleum on the cemetery grounds. Burial takes place in the spring, with no additional ceremony except perhaps for immediate family.

— *Diane Lee Moomey*

Suburbs, Chapparal

The Red Hour

Not an hour, not truly, not even
half. In fact, she nearly
missed the whole show by turning seaward,
entranced by that westering sun
just sliding behind the water,
nearly missed red, hoping
to catch the green flash they talk about.

The red hour,
not an hour though the earth
does stop for a breath or two, stops
while the eucalyptus grove
on the other side of the coast road
turns that Maxfield red, that copper-filled gold
so loved when art was still nouveau;
stops while that red sweeps silently
from trunk to tops, grays into dusk.

And she would have missed red,
but for a noise from the road behind her
— a shout, the slam of a car door—
a suddenness that turned her face, frowning,
to the east.

And there it was . . .

Dirt. Just dirt.

Above the spare tire
but below the blower and its orange cord,
among pruning shears, dog treats and bags
of bone meal; beside the hula hoe
and the bottle holding emulsion of fishes,
its cap askew, dockside scent wafting
over all . . . in there somewhere is a set
of knee pads: Blue nylon, foam-filled,
velcroed fore and aft.
Queenly knee pads.

   I could go get them.

Already these knees in less-than-denim,
in gray and blue striped once-pajama
bottoms nearly bare of thread,
already these knees have sunk
deep into loam, are cradled in cool
beneath this loropetalum,
among the spotted spurge.

   Weed: green-growing
   where I did not intend, and faster
   than it has a right to.

I could, this April afternoon—
the too-warm, too almost-summer,
three-pm-lazy stillness
broken only by the *wahwahwah*
of the mow-and-blow downstreet—
I could and probably should climb
that pergola and snip brown heads
from Lady Banks' rose but oh! the shade
beneath the loropetalum! And the spurge,
the dandelion and wild strawberry
crowding rudely the helleborus!— quite
rudely! And so I remain, slide wet knees
further between the branches.

   No one can see me.

4

I pluck, toss each weedling on the walk.
A red worm, freed from the walls
of her self-made tunnel, thrashes
in air. I scoop a hollow
into last year's leaf mold, drop her in.

A privet has trespassed— tall. I pull.
Its root mass, tough and too large
for its top, lets go
in a spray of soil and scent.

> *Dirt. Just dirt.*
> *I press that root ball to my nostrils.*

The old smell:
Suddenly I am two, set down in the garden,
briefly unwatched, a private silent moment
engaging the scents of my world, aromas
yet unnamed as I cannot now name
layers in a bouquet of chocolate, or speak
of how this bar differs from those,
except that it does, and all
are chocolate.

> *Loam. Soil. Earth. Marl. Glebe. Alluvium.*
> *All dirt.*

Once rock. Before that, molten rivers
far below what was not yet our feet;
Before, free atoms in the hearts of stars.
It was.

Whump! A car door.
My client has returned. She'll see
boot soles protruding from the shrubbery,
green piles on the walk and know
I am doing something horticultural
most competently.

> *She will not see the dirt on my nose.*

I am not an Early Riser

The red dog of morning
sweeps daily through my window
between the second round of dreaming
and the third, nuzzles my pillow
to see if today is the day
I will open more than one eye.

Ears forward, lip corners turned up
in what could be a smile were she human,
she waits in case I push away the duvet, stand
and, without coffee, follow her.

Waits.
But this eye has closed again,
(always this eye closes again).
She turns her back
and, toenails clicking across the kitchen floor,
continues her red route west.

Ode, on realizing
that five of my best poems were born
doing Sixty on Two Eighty between Page Mill
and Sand Hill

It's the Dish.

That metal ear plucks news from the Nebulae:
baseball scores from Betelgeuse,
what they're wearing on Altair,
the latest on Strings.

    Some waves never die.

That Dish, smelling of static,
warps its own space— sonnets and villanelles,
lambent, leak from heavenly fissures.
Egrets, one-legged, contemplate haiku
and cows surround, pantoum-moo
with bovine grace.

    Stanfordians circumambulate.

The Dish.
News from the Nebulae,
the best of Orion's open mics
and, rebounding off the cosmos' curving walls,
the syllables of bards long gone
returning to shatter our firmament
all over again.

Creating the Worlds

In the first world the sun
rose only every other day and the moon
fell from the sky because
the gravity module worked
in theory only. Tenants refused
to move in, so the first world
was compost.

The next was an improvement although
the second-generation gravity module
slipped a disc and everything fell sideways.
The tenants complained because
whatever they dropped the neighbors got
and drapes were all soaked through,
though it *was* written in the lease
to keep windows shut during stormy
weather— not so much to ask.
They moved out and the second world
was toast.

The third was nearly perfect until
the icemaker jammed and froze
the planet solid at both poles
halfway to the equator. Most of the tenants
moved out in protest, still owing rent.

It would have been a crime
to jettison a world so nearly perfect
so the Powers agreed to thaw it out
and try again. Tenants returned but this lot
smoked and fought over everything
including the thermostat—
the icemaker couldn't keep up.
All the carpeting had to be re-created
and they moved out anyhow.

The fourth world will be non-smoking.
Would-be tenants are picketing but everyone knows
this is the only world in town. This time around
the Powers agree to keep the red and the blue
on separate continents, and to confiscate that
internal combustion engine they are all so fond of.

The fifth world is still on the storyboard.

Too Long a Gardener

With curse and furrowed brow do I regard
the mole's swift progress 'cross the verdant turf;
I shriek and thus repulse the thieving jay,
cast stones and nets upon the cherry trees;

the inchèd worm, leaf green, the long delight
of those my salad days, its curving length
borne gracefully 'twixt toes both fore and aft,
alas now only brings my shudd'ring gasp
and reaching for the vessel which does hold
elixir, juice of "Safer," noxious spray —
does send that worm to its too-early grave.

     Forsooth have I too long a gardener been.

Oh, leaf and bough bedecked with noisome scents
unseemly rank, and yet most sore in need
if Bambi shall be banished from her deeds;
oh, bough and leaf replete with aphid herds
so tender, plump and green, close tended by
their shepherds: ants, the ants, the ants, the ants, . . .

The hopeful purchase of red ladybugs—
I plead with them to stay, to savor long
what lies so amply spread before their eyes—
but oh, uncanny swift do they depart
to feast upon the greensward 'cross the way,
and gambol midst my neighbor's roses, so
the spray, the spray, the sorry, sorry spray!

Perchance in days of my antiquity,
enfeebled limbs arranged in rocking chair
beside my many-gophered lawn, I'll lunch,
observe with mild indulgence how the deer
partakes of ev'ry rose, and how the worm,
that fine green worm weaves tents among the plums,
how flop-eared rabbits midst my cabbages
make sport; I'll gaze with fondness on the jay,
each cherry nipped, and on fair crow that plucks
each new-sown seed from out the lettuce bed.

    Perchance this happy end, perchance— but nay,
    for far too long have I a gardener been.

Give Me Maps

I'll search for you, MapQuest or Yahoo;
print out words to send me
spiraling to your front door, eventually.

I'll Google, click "satellite", note
the color of your mailbox; your boat,
how many dandelions in the yard.

Instruct my 'droid
to call out, in loud voice,
male or female my choice, to
"turn left at next intersection,
   turn left at next intersection,
      turn left at next intersection."

I'll do these things with grace for you,
but oh for pure adventure, do
give me maps, give me paper, give me maps!

Give me ink: new, or with piney residue
of picnic tables past. I'll unfold their vasty beauty,
fill the dashboard, fold, behold
the North and South of them, the scale of miles;
drop mustard onto Wichita,
count inches to Vancouver,
Cheboygan, Dubuque.

Give me maps!

And children who'll demand
while dripping jam on Alabama, will demand—
of course they will demand— to know
if we are There yet.

Raising Bread

First this: winter wheat,
whole wheat, hard wheat;
grind fine.
Honey, butter, water.

    Yeast.

Then rolling, thumping,
live dough humping
beneath the fingers.

    The yeast.

Soft ball, buttered ball,
buttered bowl, tea towel atop,
white towel atop, the warm kitchen.
You did your part.

    Go away.

Yeast does not need you now. Go,
do a crossword, wash the dishes,
wash the dog, wash your hair.
Don't come back till boozy air
drifts up the stair,
beneath the bathroom door.

Pummel again, make loaf,
cover.

    Go away. Yeast
    will do the rest.

Ode
to one pound of crystalized orange peel
enrobed in Ghirardelli's Dark, or
why we must have Chocolate

I

When the plate is large
and nearly empty, the table
set down in the midst of fields
laid bare by wind, by war, by sheep;
when the morsel that does appear
on that rough plate is bitter beyond
the taste of gall; when we are living
in the weather and must
eat anything or die, then no wonder

we follow the bee,
climb her tree and fool her
with smoke, fool her and steal
her waxy sweet food, lick it
from our own fingers grown thin
by too many years of gleaning.

Once, in a winter that did not end,
we ate our own shoes.

When we must fight with jackals
over the hard crusts
that will keep one of us alive
and the other not, must dip in honey
that crust and all the husks
one can barely swallow,
then no wonder we climb other trees,
shake down the pods, ferment and roast,
make them smooth and brown
and mix them with that honey, drop in
the bitter rinds of orange.

II

When we of more auspicious times, born after
bowls of dust turned green again, born far
from fields fouled by the mongrels of war;
when our very cells remember
eating the feet of chickens;

we who shop our brief lush garden
(those dewy hillocks of pomegranate,
of kale, of bananas in winter!)
we lucky ones
who have the privilege of tossing
the ugly bits; when we recall
that locusts may again appear
in the arugula, wolves in the parking lot,

then we steer our carts (no wonder
we steer our carts!) past the dish soap
and paper napkins, past the butter
and sensible beans and as salmon
search out their own birth waters,
so do we seek asylum in the aisles
where lie the sanctuary of the Drostes,
the reliquaries of the Rapunzels and the Lindts,
the basilicas of the Scharffenbergers,
and of the Godivas.

The Houseguest Remembers

Ancient couple
twirls across the kitchen floor
to their own music.

Dinner—
he offers her a choice bit
from his own fork.

My midnight errand—
their open bedroom door.
Two heads upon one pillow
breathing the same air.

Love at the Laundromat

One for each quarter, her tears;
her dollars change with silvery *clinks*
into the pot below the spout.

  Who will keep the flat?

An orange box tumbles into the tray;
his frowns, his quarters. His fingers
hover above the buttons—
Tide. All. Breeze. Another
Tide joins the first one.

Towels, sheets, detergent, quarters,
slamming lids, separate newspapers, distant seats,
their housebreaking suspended for the nonce
though the mother-of-three
wasn't even listening, the boy with the earbuds
wasn't listening.

It takes two to fold a sheet.
More quarters, the clink of dimes,
the spinning of yellow sheets,
green towels; the tumbling, stopping, folding—
it takes two. Corner to corner,
finger to finger, not looking at him.
Corner to corner, not looking at her he says

  Let's not buy new sheets.

Finger to finger,

  Let's go home. Don't cry.

And so they don't, and they do, and she doesn't,
not for awhile anyway, and that's
just about that.

Love on Ice

Thanksgiving.
Early ice across the state line,
white ice, grey ice. A low sky
segues into ground without a pause;
blue sign points the turnoff
for Mount Saint Helens.

The California boy is driving, driving.
It's her car and he is driving, they take turns
on this trek from Santa Cruz
to Seattle; the SoCal boy is driving
and soon will have them wheels up
in the burdock. So new and polite,
she will not tell him how
to drive on ice.

He bites his lips. They slide, his polite
gives way to snipes about the tires,
the shoddiness of Fords. Her car,
the only car on this houseless road,
sure to plunge nose down in milkweed,
and stay there, the cellphone
not yet a gleam in Motorola's eye.

He skids them to a ditch-close stop.
"You drive!" They swap.

The Yankee girl selects "Drive One,"
invokes the gods of winter, the goddesses
of Maine, New York, Ontario, the tiger
whose paws she saw advertising
some brand of tire or other.

This tiger rides low to the ground, steps out
one paw at a time, melts ever so slightly
the ice beneath; hairs grip, tiger purrs,
heater purrs, he purrs. Tires circle.
It snows for forty miles.

They never did see the mountain.

Double De-Clutch, or
Everything I needed to know about the Bardo
I learned from the Land Rover

"Revs up, no, higher!
Watch your tach. That's it, in with the clutch,
good, good— no, revs are dropping,
give it gas!"

> Gas. Engine roars, wheels coast,
> head bone is not connected to
> the neck bone.

"Into neutral, yes yes,
let out the clutch, not so fast
not so fast, no, *leave* it out!
More gas, good, good, good."

> Neutral, null, no-place, void. Gearbox
> rests in suspended animation,
> the thigh bone unconnected
> to the leg bone, shin bone, ankle bone,
> hear the word of the lord.

"Watch your tach, clutch in,
give it gas, no, *more*; into second,
there you go, more gas, let out the clutch
not so fast, dammit *dammit*! okay,
clutch in again, gas, neutral, clutch out,
gas, clutch, third, gas, clutch, gas,
neutral, gas, clutch!"

> The old life has passed, new one not begun,
> driveshaft spins, empty; planets spin in space.
> Hands and feet and eyes engaged,
> semis crowd the center line,
> only the steering wheel is mine.
> Arm bone unconnected
> to the shoulder bone, hear the word
> of the Lord.

"Fourth!"

Sleeping in the Desert

*And so, says my friend, this friend of a friend of a friend buys
a cactus, and in her living room this cactus starts to shake and
shimmy and generally carry on, so she calls the nursery people
who call the grower who calls UC Santa Cruz and behold
the botanist says, "get thee out of the house," and they do and
the cactus explodes and sprays baby scorpions all over the
draperies and the shag rug. That what she said, my friend.*
                                   —from an urban legend

I might, on entering even a stranger's house,
infer her family from the shoes by the door,
from the layered scents of years of coffee
and shampoos, of smoke or its absence;
might by noting the magazines,
the wallpaper, the china, hear
the family voice, the cadence and idioms.

   I do not know You this well.

Your night— its rustlings and callings,
its movements— sends ripples
across my blue nylon. I shrink
into my center, zippered tight.

Your daylight— touching nothing but my stove,
water jug, coffee, mug, I watch
for snakes and fireants, wrap pants close,
with wary eye regard your great saguaro
for signs of labor.

   *The desert fathers lived in Your places,
   not because God abides here and not elsewhere,
   but because here is where God may be heard.*

I'll sleep on your playa tonight,
tomorrow too, on my way
from there to here, but I *could*
pause my journey, stay on
while your weathers turn full circle,
could listen to the secrets of lizards,
seek the Divine among the yucca.

I could— and one day I'd know you
well enough. My bare feet
would part the waves of biting ants,
fingers could tell from the faint humming
which rock hides the scorpion, I'd know
how to scoop the sand just so, so water rises
to my searching lips.

I *will* know you well enough—
snakes will make bracelets
around wrists and ankles, scorpions
will ride my toes.

   I won't be afraid.

The Lake Effect

Mud into Stone

Afternoon.
Wild mustard blows, morning glory
vines, twines over brief metal roof,
pink chimney, a yellow brick chamber.
Were it empty I could fit inside,
would sit inside— it's cool inside— look out
on summer corn and far-off cattle.

> *I fire*
> *You fire*
> *He, she, it fires*

Instead, inside, cups and platters,
planters, mugs and fountains nestle,
stack, balance, fill the dusty arch,
inside. Mud waits
to be turned to stone.

> *We fire*
> *You fire*
> *They fire*

Evening.
The sentry cones, clay fingers
set inside, in front of my spyholes, fire-windows.
Bricks— the yellow, the pink, all in place,
bricks all in place, neat, tight, row on row.
What have I forgotten?

The long match, hiss of gas, smell of gas—
the pilot will warm the chimney. Crows
could perch there for the night.

> *I go indoors to dream of magma.*

Morning. The chimney. No crows.
A gentle heat haze shimmies,
makes wavy the sumac across the fence.

The hush, farmlands at dawn.
The hush!
I hesitate, hand on the wheel

that opens the venturis, breaks
the silence of day. I hesitate,
turn it, brace for the rush, the suck of air,
the backflash as gas engages, as flame
circles the chamber, seeks the sky.

I finish coffee, sweep the porch,
weed a row of radicchio.

Carbon from primordial ferns
turns to smoke, the smell of swamps burning.
I open my spyhole— cups and bowls,
the cones' three fingers all backlit, black lit,
a shadow-puppet play, all red behind.

At the wheel, I throw three pots,
think about volcanoes.

Noon.
The red dwarf flares within.
Beads and planters orange—
the weather within! Red wind
whips 'round the cones. Cobalt's
once-pink powder will be turning blue.

I lie in the tall grass, eat chips,
count ladybugs.

Afternoon.
Now yellow inside as solstice sun,
bricks have swollen, stand apart.
Black copper will soon be red.
I push the damper in— small flames
creep from every crack. I cannot sit still.

At the wheel, more pots. These spatter
against the wall.

Suppertime.
Cones— first finger down.
With asbestos gloves I slide
a red-hot plug

from the upper spyhole:
flame raptors leap, go for the eyes—
a hissing, forelocks now a-crisp.
Beyond, the gleam of new glass, as atoms
give up allegiance to old molecules,
take new partners.

Someone brings salad, a glass of wine.

Evening.
Second quarter moon rising,
second finger downing. Above the glove,
arm red with burn. Impatience,
impatience. Second finger down.

The roaring, the roaring!

Midnight.
Third finger bending: Done, done,
more than done— close valve,
close chimney, silence air.
One last look at the magma within,
ears still ringing. Stone
will not return to mud.

Sounds of the night return—
peeper frogs, the slam of a car door,
music, a question from the house.
I'll salve my arm, cut my burnt hair—
three days to wait . . .

I fire
You fire
He, she, it fire
We fire
You fire
They fire

Hens

No one will be home.

Mailbox snaps free, crosses Queen Street—
empty street, glazed street— sideways,
swept away by lake wind, sudden wind,
bearing ice.

The henhouse door is open.

Traffic lights swing, blink yellow, my bus
slides curb-close on this Edward Hopper
street where later a sheet of plate glass
will flex loose from a penthouse window,
smash to glitter on the center line.

You should stay in town tonight, they'd said.

The snowplows flash yellow,
my bus behind: York Mills, Thornhill.
The warm within, out front the white,
cold and yellow, flashing, only those.
The hours.

But the henhouse door is open, I'd replied.

Now my driveway, driver peers with dismay
at its quarter mile, already thigh deep:

Will you be alright?

I will be . . . I push past
the lower pasture where fireflies
sleep out the winter. The silence,
then howling of the lake wind.

*The dog may be at home,
but no one will be home.*

I fear to find the signs
of death across my path— feathers
in the snow, the blood,
the prints of dogs and foxes.

The henyard— open door,
the drifts, the brooding boxes, drifts,
the silence, my fear
of still, cold breasts.

I step inside before I can invent
a reason not to, plunge my hand
into the snowy feathered dark:

> *one, two, three, four, five, six, seven, eight*
> *beating hearts.*

Cloud to Cloud

North of Niagara and east, north
of the peach belt and the Great Water.
High summer storm light— the undersides
of leaves flash silver in the ground wind,
that back-handed wind that gusts
now north, now west, startling
birch and aspen poplar. Crows
perch low and on the inside, rabbits
run to ground.

Waiting.

Wide lightning, pink lightning
strokes along massed cumulonimbus
strobe fully half this twilit sky— dry.
Cloud-to-cloud, never touching
ground, this lightning—
the day long and restless,
sullen heat gathering in great chunks,
going nowhere— the dry crackle that cries
for thunder. Us waiting for the deluge,
the drops that will settle the day's dust,
drenching gusts that will bring the cat
mewling to the door.

Back-porch waiting for that front
to sweep north off Lake Ontario,
to wash clean the sidewalks
and the Don Valley Parkway, to carve rivers
in the dirt on the windows
of the last subway car of the day; to come

north, make soggy the putting greens
of the Bayview Country Club,
to douse us here, porching,
way up past Markham in the true country,
in the green belt that cradles Toronto
in wide arms. Us, waiting.

Dry and waiting, holding hands
just holding hands; talking, just talking,
mind to mind, cloud to cloud,
our lightning never touching ground.

Waiting for our weather to move in,
to wet our skins, crack
our dry spell.

Barley, Corn

That was the summer we danced naked
around the silo they never used,
(*our beads, our smoke*),
our rented farmhouse an island,
corn waves tickling our shoreline— danced naked
while the growers of corn
flew low and dusted.

That spring Ralph Palmer and his sons
harrowed up, furrowed down, put
a hundred acres into barley. It was early,
and winter, not knowing its place, returned
for four days to plunge the red line to thirty,
to twenty nine, to thirty one. Barley
dies at twenty eight and on the third day
Ralph's heart stumbled and fell.

    His dog howled all night.

That was the summer we ran naked
between the rows, ate his fingerling ears,
thought *it's feed corn, not table corn,* thought
the cows won't know if they're a dozen ears short.

    That's what we thought.

Ralph lived on and so did his barley.
That was the summer we danced naked
on the lawn and I wondered when Ralph Palmer
last danced naked on the lawn,
before corn drew his life into neat furrows,
into terrible furrows. When, or if. I wondered
if corn came to him in his cradle,
if barley tapped him on the shoulder
at high school graduation and said
come with me, boy.

    That sometimes happens.

Fireflies

You'd drive me home the long way
through Nobleton and Kleinburg,
their window-dark houses— our own
windows down, our summer dark,
its colorless moon— my lower meadow
thick with fireflies, their green ghostlight,
the listless complaints of cricket frogs.
You'd stop the engine, stop the frogs.
Dark wingtips brushed our cheeks,
humming;

we'd speak of angels and the where of them.

You'd drive me home the short way
through Unionville and Markham—
the vee-dub's meager heater,
our winter-tight windows,
their ice mandalas— the meadow thick
with ice and silent, starry dark above,
You'd turn in— the snowplow
would've already been by— you'd stop
at the house, engine running. In starry dark

we'd speak of space and wonder if auroras are alive.

The night your father died,
before his time, before his time, alone you drove
the long way, the short way, the long way,
up the long drive, knocked. I opened,
and we spoke of nothing at all, only
held on and remembered
that somewhere there must be fireflies.

When I waved your car down the road
for what would be the final time, corn blades
trembled in the wind of your passing.

Deciduous

The turn of the year— empty trees,
the delicate bones of hills behind,
the black and the white of these—
empty lake, canoe, us,
our leaf-bare winter.

I take the bow, as always,
and you the stern; the dog between,
as always, always.

> *Only the loons are talking.*

Maple paddles not touching
the sides— no splash, only
dripdrip off the blade— stroke,
stroke. As if by magic
we change sides all at once.

> *We do this well together.*

Day's end— a beaver's tail slaps,
a fish twitches a phantom strider
from the circle of the moon's reflection;
antlered head appears far out,
small vee-wake shimmies with its crossing.

Day's end— our camp, our do-si-dos,
our wine. Sleeping bags and books,
the long dark.

> *Only the loons are talking.*

The chill, our frosty breath,
perhaps we'll have no spring.
Morning, breaking ice to make coffee;
low sky and whitecaps promise heavy weather.

> *This, at least, we did well together.*

Spring Breakup

We'd put in at the boat ramp,
not at the grocer's dock, though that was closer,
paved lot shaved smooth. We put in at the ramp,
and not that our boat or any boat
was going out that day— lake ice thick,
two feet or three, shore to shore.

The ramp—
its gravel lot was full of snow.
The dog, first out the door, peed steaming yellow
and flung herself from drift to drift.

Full of snow, and easy, the ramp slick and easy,
easy, and so our toboggan load of weekend kindling
and charcoal, of romaine and olives— the olive oil
already in the cabin and clouded with cold—
of milk and steaks and onions,
of red wine and dog kibble slid
like hot butter down to the lake.

We were new. The toboggan was red,
its poly ropes yellow, and we took turns
pulling. The wind! In the middle, ice
was bare and clear— we lay down,
pressed our noses to it, looked for fish
or something, and marveled that we
walked on water.

Two days, three, solid to the touch:
fire and wine, no sign of melt to come.
But we, fresh to this country,
did not know its seasons.

Dropped Stitch

Knit one, purl two.

Another sweater, begun as if it were
for him, as if it could ever be for him,
as if he would wear it, ever,
as if he would see it, ever.

The knit and purl— angora of her life,
the jute of her life— the sweater begun
because the screen door has slammed
for the last time and there is
nothing more to say.

Purl one, knit two.
Yarn over, yarn under.

Last news of the evening: on Wall Street
a crisis looms. Somewhere in Saskatchewan,
a jury is deadlocked.

Red wool, white wool.
Tessellation of loop into loop.

The Leafs have won their third
in a row. Tomorrow will be cloudy
with chance of rain.

Fumble, unravel, purl again.
Knit two purl one.

Sure as she knows that even the news
will end sometime, that the screen
will go dark and in the silence of rooms
she will be able to hear the falling of dust
as it settles on the pages of letters,

as sure as that, she knows she'd give
whatever years are left to her for a single boon:

Rip out that ruined row,
pick up the dropped stitch.

Barrow

Snow above, corn above,

small sounds of water seeping through stone,
the smell of bedrock; cave crickets,
their lightless eyes, their chittering;
small sounds, the echoes of small sound
though not of my breathing, never that,
so ragged, so light—

day above, night above—

not my breathing, now that the mourners
have gone back to their children, their rooms,
my children, my rooms, our looms,
their suppers, having first
left me a supper just in case,
because one never knows, just in case—

corn above, snow above—

having washed me, dressed me
in my best, my gold and silver;
having brushed my hair, they left me
a cold supper, just in case,
just in case I should ever

roll my own stone away.

Barking All Night

They'll bark
the stranger bark, those hounds—
nip the heels, send trespassers flying.

They'll yip the yip of a trodden tail,
or a welcome:
where the woof have you been all day!?
They'll bark all those, they will—
we will— and wag as well.

But then oh yes then
one day comes the long bark, all night
the long bark: moon-baying, savoring
the rumble in the throat, the chest.

The long bark. Lord save us all
from barking the long bark, from giving voice
across the winter-bare fields,
in vacant rooms, all night,

barking all night because
the road is empty
and there's nothing else to do.

Secrets

You told me your secrets
as someone might do
sitting beside a stranger
on a long train journey, carriage
rocking against the rails, shoulders
thumping shoulders, voices enclosed
in a quiet zone around two heads,
a private nimbus held in place
by the clacking of wheels.

You told me secrets as a person
sometimes does, knowing
that at the last stop but one
the listener will vanish
and the secrets be released into the air
of a nameless station, into diesel smoke,
the smell of railroad coffee.

You told me secrets as a man might tell it all,
knowing that at the final stop
he will debark and, down this street and that one,
find his house as he left it, knowing he need
not look back to that other station
where those secrets may already be scattered
like seed on the hard ground.

You told me secrets as if,
meeting in a foxhole, one of us
might die tomorrow.

Fauna

Hoop Drum

Night banks of the American—
Barred Owl calls *hoohoo*. I open tent flaps,
peer out into moonlessness, just in case.

Next day's trail. I stop short
at a pile of small bones, striped feathers—
hers, or her sister's. I wrap, carry
those feathers home.

Up the coast, a yellow pine
is felled and milled. Thomas Moon
buys all the straight grain—
he steams, he planes,
he curls a hoop.

Somewhere in Oregon, a brindle cow
provides a square of hide.
One wet day, Thomas
pulls it tight onto roundness,
wraps it with thongs.

These meet at the center— my hand
fits well there. I unwrap the feathers,
tie one to those crossbars.

On my hilltop,
I listen for owl, tap the drum.
In fog and fits of rain, she speaks
with hoarse voice. *Bumph.*
I bring her indoors, set her
near the fire.

Boom.
Hoohoo!
Boom.

Oyster

Lazy morning in the beds,
plankton adrift, her shell agape—
a passing flounder flicks sand,
and there it lies on the soft tongue tissues.

Mollusk lips snap shut too late,
close on the sharp
that can be neither swallowed
nor spat out—

    the flotsom, jetsam.

The sharp— no matter what size or shape,
what color— that shard will be buried
within the limey mantle, the nascent pearl.
Then years, the nacre, the years,
the core forgotten—

    a word, a look, a letter?

In small closed rooms, the dark, the tides
and currents; bivalves open, bivalves close,
the long slow spheres
grown not by choice, never by choice—
pearls simply happen.

And the oyster herself is wrapped around,
soft around, dark around and blind to
her own pearl.

July on the Coast

I may have interfered
this year, but just because
summer is not at all, here,
and spring-bloomed fuchsias
have nothing to replace them.
Hummingbirds seek in vain,
in rain like winter's.

I buy a glass bottle,
fill it with red, hang it upside
down till fuchsias bloom again.

And then a junco bird appears
where none have been for two years
or three, and peers
into my windows, hops close
as if to get a better view.

I fill a plastic bottle with millet.
The bird returns, with family,
flings seed wide in what is surely
glad abandon.

One might think I interfere
for no *because* at all, except
I see a flash of brightest yellow
downslope among the eucalyptus,
want it close and so buy

a sock filled with thistle seed—
chocolate to finches, I hear.

This morning, thirteen
yellow bellies and brown,
hang heads down,
head-to-tail spiral
around the swaying sock.

These acts— sudden gusts
in the karmic winds of birds,
appearing on cue?

Or interference?

Heron II

Gray Christmas week— my car
takes the rolling turns
of this schoolhouse road.

Sere hillside, sudden gray heron.
Expected— the silence,
waiting on one foot,
successful stab, neck lifted high.

Not expected—
never painted on silk. never
sonneted, haiku-ed or pantoumed, or even
limericked—
the gopher in its beak.

Distal Points

Beside her door, yin and yang
circle each other in black and white,
a Chinese character, brushed— long life?
Her name below, brass bell above,

    I ring.

Door opens— a drift of sandalwood smoke
mingles with the jasmine above my head.
She draws me inside. "Eyes," I begin, "my eyes ..."
"Yes," she murmurs, "yes. Now ..."

    I show her my tongue.

In two fingers, she takes my wrist
closes her eyes, listens
to what I cannot hear. "Mmmm ...
the liver is wild ... please lie down
and take off your socks."

    I lie down.

Her needles slide into ankle skin, the webs
between my toes. Belly gurgles,
cheeks tremble, I think
of my sister!

    I'll ask her a question.

My brother will answer. Turning right,
I'll find I've gone left. I'll plant seeds.

Somewhere in Andromeda,
a star will change course.

Weathers

Tornado Warning

Burning rubber. The teachers
are burning rubber. They empty
their parking lot, they corner
on two wheels, home. We gawk
from the sidewalk— *we thought
you lived at school*—we watch,
sticky hot slow, we watch
till Miss Mellon rolls down her window,
hollers to hurry and we do. Before that

they said on the PA "go home"
and before that, they got a warning
on teachers' radio, "go, go!"
and before that, the clouds looked funny
outside the library window.

Down Clover Way, our way home,
our sky billows black and green behind us.
Sister and I walk backwards, marveling. A mother
screams from her front porch "get your butts
home!" and we do.

Our mother rescues laundry,
fumbles wooden clothespins, fingers
rushing pale against a serpentine sky.
"Basement!" she hollers over the sound
of the ground wind whipping her skirt
into arcs of white and purple gingham,
"Southwest corner!"

We know southwest, tumble
downstairs with the dog, find
the lunch our mother has made, eat
pickles and ham sandwiches, wish
we had a real window down here.

Radio voices crackle,
say this twister is sliding above us,
heading for downtown Flint.

   But Nancy from church lives there.

We play Go Fish and tease the dog
as *warning* turns to *watch* and our father
shuts off the radio, to save the batteries.
Just in case, kids spend the whole sticky night
in the fruit cellar under the basement stairs.

Tomorrow he will drive us
to what used to be downtown. His eyes
will be shiny and he will bite his lip.
I will look for Nancy's street.

Tonight, we just think of southwest
and wonder if people live there.

Jacks, a Game

Onesies, twosies, threesies.
    Ten metal stars, red ball— the game
    no grown-up knows— the secret game
    girls teach to girls.

Foursies, fivesies, sixsies.
    I never saw a boy with jacks, not ever.

Sevensies, eightsies, ninesies,
    A smooth floor, a cee-ment floor,
    all we need. Sandy's porch— red-painted
    and cool, red-painted and flaking.
    We pick at those flakes between turns,
    pick idly, no grown-up to stop us.

Tensies.
    Who will begin? Flip hands
    backs to fronts, jacks atop, catching,
    catching— Who stumbles first goes second,
    we are matched— Back to front,
    front to back till I slip, jacks tinkle.

Babies, baskets.
    Onesies—toss and throw, bounce,
    scoop up one jack, two, three,
    catch the ball before the second bounce,
    easy easy that's why we call it "babies,"
    that easy, but even so Sandy
    fumbles threesies.

Ups, double-ups.
    Cicada afternoon,
    far enough from Motown to hear only
    the whistles at nine, at noon, at five—
    nothing happens now. Here,
    mothers and children alone in this curl
    of new and shadeless streets, seek
    basements and the north sides of houses.

Our little-girl legs in cotton shorts
stick fast to cee-ment porches,
shift to find the cool spots.
I drop on foursies.

Downs, double-downs.
    At five, a whistle will blow,
at five-thirty fathers' Fords and Jimmies
will turn into driveways up and down the street.
We will be called, at five.

Carts before horses. Kisses.
    At one, at two, our mothers
are indoors; mine naps with our twins.
The house rule is silence after lunch
and so jacks are at Sandy's, Sandy the youngest
whose mother does not nap.

Pigs in a pen.
    Sandy scoops her sixsies.
I lie down, sight along the outside edge,
a straight line of porches west down Miami Lane
to the corner of Cloverlawn, all our houses
hatched from the same architect's egg,
all our houses new, so new only aquas,
pinks, lime greens set us apart.
New, new— only this summer
are the squares of once-mud in front yards
spiky with new green we may not play upon;
infant lawns seeded in April by fathers
dragging rakes across topsoil,
by fathers misting daily till gray seeds split.

Snakes in the grass.
    Sevensies, hers. At the street's other end,
the swamp remains swamp despite attempts
to drain, to make sewers and streets, sidewalks;
this swamp the only green in our world,
the only wild in our world,
where we may not go.

Around the world.
      This humming afternoon.
      We are old enough to know
      what lies beneath its simple surface
      as we know what lurks beneath the bed
      and in the dark of stairs.
      Cochlea vibrating, fine hairs
      inside our ears quiver and we listen.
      Balls bounce and eights give way to nines.
      We listen, as children of other times
      and places listen in the midst of games
      for the sound of guns, and rotors.
      Our listening: for the first low notes
      as air raid sirens wind up to full voice,
      the call to duck-and-cover.

Double around the world.
      Listening.
      And, flickering beneath lashes,
      our macula— alert for the drop in light,
      the shift from blue to gray to black,
      the mammiformed sky— and us
      scooping up tensies, alert
      to the southwest, waiting
      for the downward-pointing finger,
      the funnel cloud
      that will scatter our game.

Sunday at the Boardwalk

Flat in blue swimsuit
baggy-bottomed with wet and sand,
sharp with splinters from the boardwalk,
flat and so too young to be prey—
hunting eyes follow only
the curvy ones. Me, knotted of hair,
sticky with ketchup: invisible.

The afternoon is mine.

"Don't go too far," she murmurs,
near sleep in yellow lounge, a baby
on either side, near sleep; beside her,
as if mirrors are facing each to each,
endless rows of chair and umbrella,
umbrella and chair, of mothers and fathers
blanket the gray sand.

The man in the chair beside us
sleeps beneath his newspaper.

The surf line laps my ankles, fishy foam,
then sucks away, hissing,
and sudden bubbles pock the wet,
sudden holes— *crabs live down there,*
or clams— however fast I dig,
I cannot catch one.

I do catch a sand dollar, mermaid's money,
hoping she won't mind.

The boardwalk: in the gloom beneath it
a half-hamburger lies, now the grail of ants—
their forays up its cliffs, quick-march
through bogs of mustard! The fallen comrades,
final peak, the triumph, the trumpets!
Ah.

And the man in the chair beside me
sleeps on beneath his newspaper.

Outbound

The five-forty-five wakes me—
the wail of the outbound freight
crying to go home
as in those days all trains did—
wakes me as every morning
in this summer month at Gramma's
it wakes me, and in this morning's waking
I remember and jump out of bed.

    The kitten waits on the rug.

An act of kindness, this is— Gramma's kindness,
overruling my father's frowns—
the summer kitten, one of too many
summer kittens at the farm, mine now
and I believe she will go back with me
to Michigan after Labor Day.
I think this, and no one says otherwise.

    What was her name?

I scoop her up, this too-small,
too-soon-taken-from-the-mother kitten,
cradle her, whisper, savor
our private morning silence
before the banging of water in the pipes,
the creak of stair treads
and the clatter of kettles
announce that the house is awake.

I creep to the kitchen, pour milk into a saucer,
carry it outside: blue and green morning,
sparrows work the chokecherry bush.

I do not count our days, see only
that one follows another and that
on one of these many days, the kitten
does not eat, and on the next does not eat.
And on the next, when the five-forty-five
whistles me awake she is not sitting, waiting
but lying, still asleep, eyes open.

I call out.

They crowd around, Gramma, Mother and Father,
and Gramma speaks loud over my father
just opening his mouth, speaks full
and strong so there will be no backtalk:

The kitten is sick and needs her mother.

And so to the farm, to Uncle's farm— me
in the back seat, holding the cat
in my arms— the farm where I follow
my uncle to the barn, let him set her,
still-sleeping, on the straw.

Her mother will come take care of her now.

I am led, let Aunt Myrtle give me
cookies, milk. Later I slip away, alone,
return to the barn to wait for the mother cat.

To wait.

Perhaps
it is the hush, the dust floating
in that long slant of light from the haymow door;
or the wind swirling hay across the floor;
or the smell of hay itself;

perhaps the mare's tail clouds carried just so,
or the wail of yet another outbound freight;
or perhaps it is only the buzz of flies
that tells me:

Even mothers cannot come here.

Wind

Fourth grade. Outdoors
is October, and the wind that circles
the planet whips yellow
leaves into brief tornadoes.

Indoors is no season at all: grey
and grey linoleum, smell of chalk dust,
the heads of presidents ecircling
the room. Today, the exports of Ecuador
trump all other concerns.

Bored.
One window is unlatched,
a captive thread flutters. I play
my game— book raised
to cover my face— shaping lips
around the ghost of breeze
crossing the room.

Oooh, aaah, eeeeh, aaah.

2
Recess. Empty soda bottle
in the playground. Wind blows
across the top, bottle seems to moan!
But green glass knows nothing . . .

In the band room, French horn, oboe,
ocarina have no voices, no fingers,
and yet— trills and tremolos,
as if they sing. Empty tubes: only the breather
gives meaning.

3
Canyonland.
Hoodoos in sandstone orange and tan,
those wind-made men and women,
give voice: Bass and treble rise and fall
as if they know!

Atop a red mesa, I open
arms wide, mouth wide, wind
blows around me, through me—
I seem to speak! but say nothing.

Baby Sis

Spaniel on the grass—
diapered twins astride,
each pats one end.

Mother in the armchair,
a twin on each side— hairbrushes
make ringlets, braids, Mohawks.

Argument in the bath—
whose trike is on the sidewalk? Bare bottoms
rush outside to claim it.

Family tempests: Firstborns shout,
fathers fume, and mothers;
baby dyad sings to itself, safe in its own boat.

  Ohh! ohh! ohh!

Homesteading: Winter

In the woodshed, our freezer
that year, for three days straight the deft
unwrapping of a plastic bag.
Cooked chicken disappears in bits,
dainty bits, gourmet bites.
Never raccoon, porcupine.
Never bear, dog, wolf.
Not a mouse.

Inside the kitchen door,
I lie in wait. Too cold for a camera —
today is for eyes only.
I wait.

Plastic noises, chatter, rattle.
Humming to itself, helping itself,
not hearing my slow steps, ermine
takes final bites, exits the bag,

    white, white!

and sees me. Feet stamp, surely
a temper tantrum, voice loud
with musteline rage.

Our eyes lock, and abruptly
our weather changes. A cloud
passes over our sun, wind drops,
my thoughts drop, scolding stops —
human and animal meet
in silence.

    No, I don't know why.

She sits like a cat now, tail
tucked beneath.
I want to see that tail, I whisper

    please let me see your tail,
    your little tail, please, please.

Slowly, as if against
a strong wind, the tail creeps
forward, trembles, appears fully,
whitely, tipped
with a charcoal smudge.

She trembles!

Her mouth opens wide, a yawn
too large for that face. Pause.

Pause, and then we shatter.
Her mouth snaps shut,
that ermine tail
flickers out of sight.

I never see her again.

Bob Wire

We called it that: wire strands
stretched tight between posts. Tight only
on the day it was made, tight
till we marauders pulled it up and down
in our endless forays cross-country;
down and up, working the staples loose,
avoiding, as we crossed over, those treacherous
bowknots along each strand, avoiding the owner
of this bob wire, sparing him
the sight of his fence in slow decline.

We accepted "bob wire" as the pastoral line
drawn between *yours* and *mine*; the token line,
meant to be crossed, we called it that, not
knowing then its terrible other uses.

2
On our side: Hollyhocks and beans,
corn in neat rows, juncos, crows.
Over the wire: Humps and hillocks
of tough sourgrass grown rank and tall
on the rich offerings that fall from the sky
and from Holsteins.

We'd go there, when summer afternoons
offered nothing better to do, go there
and cross over, push grass between cow lips
until the press of beasts too large, smelling
too much of alfalfa, drove us
back across the barbs.

3
Past pasture, just visible
beyond the farthest wire
and hazy with dark and distance, spruce
and the abode of bear,
of fox, of wolverine. Forbidden—
in packs, we'd dare ourselves
to prowl the edges.

4
Still farther out, the wild— beyond
the tooth and claw of bare survival,
a fence unseen, a fence of mind—

I dare not part its wires,
step through with urban mind,
gardener mind; dare not fill my pack
with tent and toothpaste, seeking.

The wild goes on without me.

Queen Anne's Lace

The milk train is already gone.

He might have held our hands— Andy's
and mine— after cereal, milk, banana,
after Gramma waved us up Water Street
and turned back to her morning.
He might have. I don't remember.

I *do* remember us turning onto Main, past
Cheney's, the post office, Locey's Feed Store,
the tracks, walking tie to tie. I do remember
the smell of old creosote, gravel
creaking beneath our sneakers. I do
remember climbing the four steps up to
the once-white station no one had used
since Sputnik.

Telegraph clicks words.
Grampa goes to answer, Andy and I explore,
not warned away from touching (nothing
left to touch). The warehouse
bare, still reeking of grain— the rich
feed smell, ghost bags piled high.
The loading dock— Queen Anne's Lace
and brown-eyed Susan push through
the cracked pavement.

Semis drive the distance now, it's they
that carry the scent of grain.

Waiting room— our footsteps echo
where no one waits. Ghosts
buy tickets, occupy wrought-iron benches,
fill cups from a big urn— was there an urn?—
eat sandwiches from paper bags, wait
for the twelve-twenty to Malone,
when the Rutland went to Malone.
Nothing to touch.

Sons and daughters of ghosts now
drive the distance in Buicks and Fords.

The clicking says a freight
will stop soon, leave a car on the siding.
Grampa calls out— come watch.

The Locey boys are here by now,
and all the Clarks— we've put our pennies
on the track for the monster wheels
to flatten, dare each other to grab them
now, now, now, chicken. Then shuddering,
the smell of hot iron and the last car
slams to a stop at the end of the spur.

Caboose-men in stripes, caps-ful of candy
for our happy palms— they toss, then wave
from high windows and hoot. The music!
Thumping our too-close eardrums,
dopplering to nothing as it slides
across the railroad bridge, past Borden's
into sumac, poplar, Queen Anne's Lace.

One day soon the benches will go
for gardens, the telegraph
for the Railroad Museum,
the waiting room floor
for kindling. Grampa knows
that one day soon the trains
will slide by without stopping because

    they keep this station open just for him.

Pine— Passing Through

Bark-rough arms spiral upward, resin grabs
at sneakered feet. Gods of air
wait at the top. Chickadees scatter
at my clattering ascent, little sisters
chatter in the lower branches.

Below, our corner of the Saint Lawrence Valley—
its granite outcrops, poor patches
of oats and milkweed between, scent of gasoline.
The balky tractors and muffled shouts
of the ones who've always lived here—
the sons and fathers, their hay,
the neat squared bales. Their radio—Tammy
stands by her man.

Also below, our rented house—
our family flock perched lightly
between these fields,
brief neighbors to Holsteins, horses.

I brush away needles and the offerings
of birds, part branches. South, the Adirondacks.
Beyond the silver Seaway, blue Canada
fills the North. In time, I will descend my perch
and move on to that very same Canada,
but not today.

The makers of hay may stay as their fathers did
or not, may move along when hay
is not enough, milk is not enough,
when sons and daughters say *enough*
but not today.

Today, the sun will set, as it does,
motors will clatter to a stop, cows
will head home without being called.
The sisters and the sons, the fathers,
will wash our sticky hands in well water,
will put our feet beneath the mothers' tables.

Today.

Turning

Water is warm, warm.
Belly down in the shallows,
nose pointed downstream,
minnows nibbling my skin,
I finger smooth pebbles, each

a world, whole.
This red one carried by birds
from New Mexico, with canyons still intact,
sagebrush wedged deep into crevices.

That one, green and gray,
mosses of old Ireland from the tombs
of queens. A black one
from the asteroid belt, flecked
with dust from the hearts of stars.

I turn to face upstream— water
fills my bathing suit, tickles me
down there.
Fingers together, my ship's prow
splits the current.

Brother, sisters splash
downstream beyond the next curve.
Cicada shrills, long—
Frost in forty days, it cries.

Yellow leaf twirls past,
light haze covers sun.
On the bank, our grownups laugh
loud at jokes I cannot hear.
Hairs prickle along my back,
my nipples stand up.

I look down again,
pick up a yellow pebble.

   Just a rock, only a rock.

Saint Lawrence Suite

Nadir

This I remember . . .

Father flees the old life—
with clouds massed dark behind
that fox runs to ground, seeks
the Valley he grew up in, seeks
to start over. We are swept along,
as children are, our "whys" unanswered.
We start over, too.

Too late, summer's end, too late
for good places, new places.
Too late, only this farmhouse left,
stair treads worn to curves. Parlor
with funeral door nailed shut,
papered shut, yellow cabbage roses.
Sixty watts throughout— we share
with mice.

The Valley he grew up in: that River
rules it, sends first snow shouting, knocking
on our door. By morning, small drifts
have come inside.

Dark red linoleum,
evening silences. Ice crystals
creep through the north wall that once
was lath *and* plaster.

Coal burns fitfully below.
Faint warm breaths hang
over wrought iron filigree
on the kitchen floor. The dog
lies on top.

Morning silences.

On New Year's Eve, the sun rose red. An icicle
hung from the kitchen faucet.

Young Man in Winter

Young men are immortal.
Young bulls prove otherwise.

A young man in winter— *I*
can handle him myself!—
takes a feed bucket in one hand,
opens a gate stiff with ice. Boots
falter, slick on ridges of packed snow.

Young bull tosses horns,
stamps feet.

A January sun shines too bright.
Tombstones lean like old teeth, neighbors
lean on each other. The preacher
speaks with confidence of God's plan.

The ground is iron.
Who could dig a grave? Six
carry that terrible box
into the shed, with the other boxes
awaiting thaw.

Candle Ice

In that month when sap rises,
when smoke rises, and steam from sugar shacks
across the great North,
when night is loud with frost, and bright
middays break water free of ice, then
lake ice begins its melt
from within. Not withering
crystal by crystal till disappearing
altogether, but washing away in a most
vertical manner, leaving candles.
Just candles. Ice candles.

We eat them like popsicles.

Not like icicles— merely roof water,
tar water, bird poop water,
though not without merit— available
all winter long, harvestable
with mittened hands.

No, these candles require bellying-down
to the dock, require
a bare-armed plunge to the elbow,
probing the still-icy waters
for a whole one, one as long as the ice sheet,
January-thick.

They taste of tamarack, of loon
and pickerel, of kayaks and canoes.

Skates

Little girls stiff in new
Christmas skates, white—
always white, our girl skates—
with silver blades and teeth
that grab. We tumble,
then find our feet.

Arabesque, the twirl, the race
to the pond's far end, the breathless
drop to ice, sliding to a stop
on blue-nylon-padded knees.

I flop onto my back.
A snowflake lands exactly
between my eyes.

Now on my belly.
Mittened fingers rub a clean place— nose
against the ice, hot breath
melts a bare spot. Cupped hands
around my eyes make a shadow tunnel.

Under that glazing, a liquid world
where surely a fish will swim
close enough to peer at me
from her side of our window.

Kiting

My skies have not seen kites since ones
we flew at ten, at twelve. We climbed
the hill, my brother and I, climbed
above the creek where snow might still
be clinging to the north sides of boulders,
climbed beyond the boggy pasture.
Holsteins looked on with mild
interest.

We lay on our backs after the first run
into wind, played out cheap cotton string,
not too fast, waiting for the first tug.
Would it hold?

It held, it always held, that string.
Holding balsa tips, awaiting the grab
of wind, the thin paper bellying,
our shouts pushing them up— up, then
we lay on our backs in the tall grass.

Rolling ocean hills, my hills today,
so very green in winter, so ochre in summer,
and nearly bare— a copse or two,
a cow or two— hills empty and round
and crying for kites but bare
of kites, quite bare of kites. Children
in my world do not kite.

Back then, mine was blue,
my brother's yellow, with tails
long and magically patterned:
strips from dishtowels worn through.
String all the way out, surely
above the stratosphere by now.

We lay on our backs, thrilled
to thoughts of sudden lightning, wondered
whether clouds could see us.

Burdock

The gray farmhouse, it was,
the one with six gables. We'd complained.

> *Only six? How could they*
> *stop so close to seven?*

You must remember:
weekly, cows burst through
their feeble fence to visit our yard—
the succulent green of it! the clover!
The lilacs and roses of it!

Two maples lived in that lawn. No, maples—
the elms were at the *white* farmhouse.

We had fireflies
and burdock across the road.
One winter I sank mittened hands
into a mass of those brown hooks on purpose.
Ma was angry.

Don't you remember? *That* house.

That day it was the burdock,
purple blossoms done, that fluttered
brown in an afternoon of no wind,
flapped and fluttered. We ran
to look. A sparrow caught fast,
wings aflap, going nowhere.

> *Surely it will die.*

You snapped the stalk.
I ran for tiny scissors. We met
on the porch.

You held, I snipped and plucked
close as I dared.
The sparrow surrendered to its fate,
did not struggle though its breast was laid
almost bare.

The last hook: You turned the bird
belly side down. It dropped
a large blue poop in your hand.
In gratitude, I believed.

We watched it fly
behind the barn, just
another sparrow.

    Surely you remember.

Death of a Stranger

One afternoon in winter, I heard
that you had died.
I did not know you, except for brief nods
at the post office, the grocery.

There was snow, I recall— brief and wet,
seen crookedly through farmhouse glass slumped
with age— and a pale yellow band that divided
two grays from each other, in the west.
I thought the sun might be somewhere
behind the yellow although
there was nothing to prove it.

I remember snow
and that a car drove south along the farm road,
a red car, slushed to the hubcaps,
and that wind blew as it always does
straight down from the Saint Lawrence River,
a feral wind that pushes aside
the feathers of down jackets,
seeking the bone. Old thistles, milkweed,
barley grass, and other summer leftovers
lay flat before it.

I remember that sugaring had begun
and that the pond was smooth and white
with empty ice beneath.

I did not know you.

Memorial Day

Father and mother and me
drive to Dickinson, to Chazy
and Champlain, where our dead remain:
with potted mums we pay homage
on their granite doorsteps.

Drive past Holsteins and new corn,
where deep in Dutchman's pipe we find
his once-screened porch,
her summer kitchen, his head-high hedge
once clipped and mown— their former homes
now other-owned, or burnt,
or gone to dock and chicory.

     We do not bury our houses when they die.

Don't look, she cries. He had hydrangeas
all along that fence. *Don't look.*

A fruit cellar. *Was it hers?* Just the cellar,
wild berries now twined around
their cousins in tumbled jam jars.

The graveyard visit was the easier.

Family Secret

The cave of childhood. Shadows play across the entrance,
their sources unseen; sounds echo from wall to wall,
sounds that may have meaning or not, while the secret
lives of fathers and mothers continue.

1
Sleepless pillow— she overhears
words not meant for young ears.
Sparse words as if, climbing attic stairs,

she'd opened dusty drawers, read scraps
not hers to read. These burrow deep,
enter dreams.

2
After midnight, after peeper frogs,
long after neighbors have closed
curtains and lights

it comes— the knocking.
Soft, a heavy hand in leather glove
knuckling her door. Always
she must open.

Dark hats low, collars high,
faces in shadow—
she knows they frown.

Three.
Always there are three—
they frown.

On the porch, well wrapped:
what they've brought for her to bury
and she must, lest
the pile grow and someone notice.

3
Sleeping mysteries will not lie.
Now grown, she asks *what, why?*
but family eyes slide sideways,
silence rings like bells.

They will *not* lie, and as the tongue
harangues the aching tooth she probes,
seeks doors, seeks drawers,
closets that may hold the secret's other half—
hopes to know, dreads to know.

To know . . . but by now, perhaps,
that skeleton has no bones.

Family Reunion

Butter passed, potatoes passed,
and peas. The roast, the salad.
The talk— casting lines downstream
into the river we've named our past.

"I remember this," and tell the tale.

What I tell—
its coinage, color and shape, tone
and time of happening—
has no importance. Consider it only one
of a thousand moments-of-family
played out in every place and time, of no importance
except that I've remembered and brought it
shyly to our late-in-life table.

> *"Oh, no."*
> *"No, I never did that."*
> *"She never did that."*
> *"You dreamed it."*
> *"Never. Oh, no, no."*

Well.
I could doubt myself,
call myself forgetful, blurry of mind,
claim mistake and cast the recollection
back into the family river,
but

I *do* remember, it *did* happen, did.
I step back, silent,
hold the fragile droplet close—
I know you, I was there—

and guard it, as with open palm
I would guard a candle's flame
from the gusts of unknowing winds.

Brave

Two a.m., too late for owls—
Mallet and chisel, chisel and mallet,
shoulders ache, ache; mallet and chisel, slip
and cut, blood on white marble—

I entered it anyway— the ladies
gave it a ribbon and called me brave.

At dawn I filled pages, then read
to listening eyes and watching ears
the poem that shook me awake at three,
told secrets, secrets—

they called me brave.

He'd struck me once, twice, once
too often, too often, left marks.
The day of my leaving

she called me brave.

My slingbacks, blusher, kohl-dark eyelids;
my curled gray head the only one
in a ballroom blonde, redheaded, brunette . . .

the ladies called me brave.

Exuent

Burning at Both Ends

They say that
like it's a bad thing, like
that double flame ain't just the *best*
you'd ever want, and you not knowing anyway
whether you're gonna last longer
with only one end lit— you'll maybe
get hit by a bus before you can even
vote, and they'll pry that half-a-candle
from your rigored fingers.

It ain't like your kid
or your brother
or your dog
can use what's left, and that's a fact.

And they say it like there's only one
handed out, ever, right along
with your first diaper and that's it,
the box and the matches
snatched away forever and that may be so,
it may be so.

But I say it ain't a *bad* thing.

Diminuendo

Perhaps better that your body died.
Perhaps better that you lay flat
and still on pavement like the shattered
windshield of last night's head-on.
Perhaps better that than this
long slow slide into the gathering dark.

If your body had died then I could
wash you and lay you out upon your bed
and sit beside you for the three days.

We always sit beside the dead for three days
because they might, just might, after two days
and twenty-three and one-half hours,
sit up again and say, "Where are my shoes,
and why am I wearing this?"

They hardly ever do, but they might.

You did, did not, die.
Another one looks out the eyes
that were yours once.
I don't want to know him.

I've called for you.

You did, did not die. You keep
talking about something.
I fold my coat close around me,
hold my body taut against this cold.

Death is death, I suppose,
whether of body or mind or heart
or love or fame or illusion,
and its naked fact is scarcely
to be believed; the *nowness* of it
scarcely to be believed.

On the screen death comes
with its own music, lighting—
the single spot, the slow pan, zoom
to the face, the diminuendo.

It's over. Now. Boom.

In midnight rooms, no music except
the humming of blood in our own ears,
the awful hiss of breath. Hours
of waiting, the walls dissolve, the boat
pulls away from shore, hours.

Is this it? Now? Was that it?
We want to know these things.

You did, did not, die
and I am still on your doorstep,
not in, not out.

The Smell of Horses

As you lie dying, incredibly,
rain keeps falling,
snow melts, there is new grass
and the smell of horses,
their soft *chuff!*, stamping of feet,
nuzzling of pockets for treats.

Then the shrieks of naked children
who do not know, who go on
summering and porpoising
in plastic backyard wading pools,
their dogs driven mad with joy
at so much noise and water. As if
nothing extraordinary were happening,
which is as it should be.

Months compress into hours, a day
requires a full year to pass,
and now and again, time
stops altogether.

You called me your rock, once.
We laughed, then, about whether I was
granite, or rose quartz,
or perhaps amethyst.

Today I hold a geode, that marvel
of crystalline engineering, the round
black boulder, so quiet, so plain; the shocking
lining of purple. I roll it over
and over in my palms, slide fingertips
along the points, waiting
for the phone to ring. Time stops

altogether, then with an almighty
grind, starts up again. Suddenly
autumn crocus are in bloom,
and chrysanthemum— ragged,
rust red and sharply golden— as if no one
ever lay dying.
I pick a handful, then another.

Hours pass— shredded petals fill my lap.

As you lie dying: A low sky
and the smell of warm snow hovering
on the doorstep between ice and water.
Warmth or cold determine whether I see
solid, liquid, gas. Somehow
this seems important.

You ask, I bring
a squeezed fistful, not quite a snowball,
and set it on your upturned palm.
We sit quietly watching it melt:
ice, water, gone.

Café
long after the funeral

At the next table, coffee
with his two lumps, two
cuplets of cream.

Flannel shirt
crumpled carelessly upon a chair seat:
his colors.

Cast-off napkin folded
and folded and folded again,
his tea-shop origami.

Loves Lost, Loves Found

The Body Speaks,

no need to be told how. Infant body
watches— each year carves learning
deeper into cells.

Grown body
speaks without speaking:
the crossed arms, the open arms,
the arms akimbo,

the crossed legs, the tapping foot,
the swinging foot,
the shrug, the shaken finger,
the Finger.

The smile and the frown.
The head: the nod "yes," the shake "no."
The shake from side to side, slight rocking:
"Maybe, but probably not."

The innocent body knows
its own dance, the glossary
of Home, knows not
of knowing only one until waking
one day in Kathmandu.

He shook his head. "Yes,"
he'd said, but I heard "no"
and walked away.

Precious

Precious.
not *master*, not *sir*, but
precious.
We call you that.

Now we ask
not who are you, but *what*?

Transparency.
The faintest outline only,
as the skin of bubbles blown from a child's pipe:
only that marks
the space we love to call *you*.

Within that space, what?
Really, what?

Nobody's in there, and yet
there's light, sometimes, or heat.
If I am asked again *What*
and pressed for a reply I will say that.
Light only, or heat, nothing else,

and *clear*,
your presence a pause in the daily news.
An iris, and seen through that iris
a range of impossible peaks.

And occasionally seen, midnight rooms,
where alien couples, naked,
make love
by the light of multiple moons.

I have maps, but your Name is not on them

I saw you once— you breached
in front of me, breached and fluked and dove again.
Your eye! Your eye!
I tossed my latté, quit my job.
At the tideline, I ate kelp and waited.
My hair grew long. One day I knew that water
does not leap into the mouth of the thirsty one.
I begged a boat.

> *Onshore were crowds*
> *and well-wishing, cheers, a champagne launch.*
> *I waved, untied my lines.*

Alone on open ocean,
masts creaking— I took on water.
What to do with that horizon? endless sky?
the silent cloudy nights?

Far from the shipping lanes, from time to time
I'd meet another. We'd search each other's eyes—
Have you found it?— share charts, move on.

> *I had maps, but your name was not on them.*

Now my restless prow swings
to Polaris, the Southern Cross, and back again—
you're out here somewhere.
I'll breathe water, I'll live here, swimming
in the Ocean where you are.

> *I have maps, but your name is not on them.*

Compass twirls— I've sailed too far north
or south. Empty nights, empty lights:
aurora's hum carries no message.
My cold, the winter sea—
ice boulders batter my hull.
Breached, I beach on clean sand—
nothing to do but wait here, for your lightning
to strike again.

I Have Always Been Your Lover

Now is not our time.
other promises press close, insist
on being kept.

I am your lover.
in unseen places, we live together.

We talk,
but not of this— other words
fill the space between us.
Strange, how the unspoken ones
lie sweetest on the tongue.

Before there were planets anywhere,
I was your lover.

I remember visiting
a place of geysers,
of sleeping volcanoes.
cool forest lay above
and beneath, the slow steady boil.

The molten core:
no life without this.

I will always be your lover.

Seven Love Poems

1
My beloved and I
enter the room where Love is
and put ourselves,
like presents,
into that One's lap.

Babies
give, take back,
give, take back:
We all start out that way.

Love waits,
until the gift is given
for keeps.

2
We went to Love's house:

We were honey
and milk
and eggs
and flour.

Love beat us and baked us
and made a cake of us.

Those who ate it
tasted cake:
not honey
or milk
or eggs
or flour.

3
We fell in love,
we fell into Love,
and that was that.

Once in,
none walks away
from that terrible gentleness.

Once in,
none is untouched
by that beloved Earthquake
that shatters
what you and I were,
before.

4
We fell into Love,
and Love
tore out the stitches,
turned the pieces
inside out,

re-arranged
and sewed them back
together again.

Now we do not remember
which ones were mine
and which ones
yours.

5

We lay so close
and so still
for so long
that we could not feel
the other's skin

and had to look
to see if we still
touched.

6

It was
such a mistake
to have put male
and female
into separate bodies.

Now we spend
all our time trying
to get back inside
the same skin.

7

When we fell in love,
when we fell into Love,
we became invisible
to ordinary eyes.

When we fell in love,
when we fell into Love
we walked the earth unseen,
as lovers have done
always.

Our Moon, Reunion

Days and nights we walked your garden.
Spent petals of camellia softened our steps.
Our moon fell and rose, our shadows
on your perfect stucco walls. Our arms
fell and rose in cadence
with our words, the perfect rhythm
of our words. Their brimming pools
flooded the parched years
of our silence.

> *When we parted, I took a stone.*

My own garden, your stone warm in my hand.
A blossom falls, finished. Wrapped
in its pink heart, one of your words.
Gardenia: saucer full beneath its pot.
I tip the water out. What spatters
on the flags is the joke you told.
Our moon rises— I hear again
the story of your dream.

Ars Poetica

Rhythm, Rhyme

Your villanelle assures the break of day,
subdues the eyes beyond the fire's light:
My sonnets hold the roofless dark at bay.

The chanting drum, our dancing feet make tame
the taloned wild; the ballad speeds the night,
the villanelle assures the break of day.

The litany, the liturgy: To pray
in chapter, stanza, verse, arrests the lightning;
sonnets hold the hungry dark at bay.

The lullaby, the fable chase away
the wolf beneath the bed, the ghouls that bite;
the villanelle ensures another day.

The wild one waits beyond the glass: Charades,
sestinas, odes, ghazals protect our lighted
rooms; the sonnet holds the dark at bay.

The rhyming lines, the pulse, cantabile,
accompanied by lute, by flute and fife:
My villanelle assures the break of day.
Your sonnets hold the roofless dark at bay.

Five Poem Poems

1
Somewhere, on no map:
a meadow where poems grow. The poet
goes there, picks some, takes them
home to be enjoyed.

Nobody owns those fields—
they're just *there*.

    2
    A poem wakes up
    in the dark, stumbles, falls
    onto paper.

    Later, it finds its feet, begins
    to dance.

3
Some of these poems
are not meant to be heard. Some
are the throw-away proof paper
off the press; some, the box
the paper came in. Some poems
are not meant even to be read.

    4
    I found a poem in the garden.
    It came up in a shovelful
    of earth, stained and muddy,
    mildew in the cracks, chipped
    around the edges.

    Potato poems! I won't dig them all
    up now. Some I'll save
    for next year's crop.

5
This poem arrived wrapped
carefully in the scrap words
of the one that came before it.

Carefully,
so as not to be broken
by rough handling.

Saturday Morning

East window,
lightly glazed with snail trails, illuminates
dust, crumbs, a week's debris, glitters
on car keys beside the back door.
Finches argue over the last
of the nyjer seed.
Need I reply to these?

Water is waiting:
Water and the whitest of paper, thick
and soft, as is the brush
of dark hairs and round handle.

Beside these, fresh pots of yellow,
of red, of the bluest of blues
in which might be found the exact russet
of the grosbeak's breast.

Brushes are waiting.
The sun in the East window
gives light for this.

Glaze

February.
Ice from bank to bank, the creek,
though water runs beneath— small bubbles
mark the current an inch from pressing fingers.
Swept along: bits of summer leaf,
wing of dragonfly.

I am so thirsty.

2
Bottle on the bathroom shelf, not
out of reach. Fat golden beads,
smooth and rubbery. How delicious
they must be, how sweet they smell!
How I push with baby fingers!
They will not pop.

I consider teeth.

3
Blank page at hand,
I wait for lightning, pen at hand, probe
for what will shatter today's flat
shine, pierce the icy glaze, prick the rubber
shell that holds the living gel—
the quick, the rolling.

I stab with pen, await the lance,
the arrow word; wait,
beseech the muses.

4
Again the beads: My mother opens
the hot tap, drops one into the water.

March rolls into April—
Again, the creek.

Waiting for a Real One

Waiting for a train, awaiting,
baggage beside her, she watches her watch
for no good reason but to show
faith: At a certain hour
that train *will* appear.

      Waiting. The station master
      does *some*thing behind a glass window,
      something she sincerely hopes enables
      the arrivals of trains

on time. In the old days she'd waited days,
ears to the rail, watching for smoke, waited
at whistle-stops— brought lunch
and dinner too, and breakfast and lunch
again, waited days.

      Not like now, not like now
      she repeats with touching confidence
      watching her watch again, shaking
      her watch— perhaps it's fast,
      or stopped.

Flukes

Robe

Three a.m.
I leave my bed
to walk the night plane,
open my robe:

wind I cannot see lifts hair,
swirls between toes. Blackness.
Even coyote
dares not come here.

I am not afraid.

I leave my bed
to swim the night ocean.
Whales take my robe, wear it
for a joke.

I will not need it.

I leave my bed,
and may be back by morning,
or not.

Whales

1

When I swam with whales,
we opened our mouths to fill ourselves
with sea, so that we
were a thin skin, with ocean
without, and ocean within.

2

It is the work of whales
to cruise, to ensure that every drop
breathed in is tasted
and breathed out again.

It is the work of oceans
to lie quiet and liquid,
and let that happen.

When I am Old

I shall live by the southern ocean
when I am old,
in a round house with
seagrass for a door.
I'll build it myself.

I shall eat kelp.

A gray cat will live with me,
a very old gray cat, indifferent
to the seabirds that will walk
upon my skin.

I shall lie at the water's edge
each day, mark the new year
by the return of gray
whales from the north.

Acknowledgments

For inspiration and guidance, thanks to David E. LeCount, Casey FitzSimons, Marvin R. Heimstra and other members of the delightful poetry community of the San Francisco Bay Area. In addition:

Thanks to *Perfume River Poetry Review* for publishing "Kiting"

Thanks to *Red Wheelbarrow* for publishing "Memorial Day, Pilgrimage" and "Barley, Corn"

Thanks to the *Sand Hill Review* for publishing the following poems: "Barking All Night", "The Body Speaks", "Sleeping in the Desert", "Dirt. Just Dirt.", "Jacks", "Our Moon, Reunion", "Pine— Passing Through", "The Red Hour", "Family Reunion", "Spring Breakup", "Outbound", "Queen Anne's Lace", "Young Man in Winter", "Diminuendo" and "The Smell of Horses".

Thanks to *Glass: a Journal of Poetry* for publishing "Fireflies"

Thanks to *The Willow Glen Poetry Project* for publishing the following poems: "Burdock", "Kiting", "Skates", "Death of a Stranger", "Ode (the Dish)", "Candle Ice", "Creating the Worlds", "Sunday at the Boardwalk" and " Turning"

Thanks to *Poetalk* for publishing "Heron II" and "The Houseguest Remembers"

Thanks to *Two-Twenty-Four Poetry Quarterly* for publishing "Whales" as "The Work of Whales"

Thanks to *Anabasis: the Love Project* for publishing "Such a Mistake"

Thanks to Carrie and Jean of the Peninsula Literary Series for choosing "Dirt. Just Dirt." and "Chocolate" to be guest-read at their quarterly venue.

About the Author

Diane Lee Moomey has lived and wandered around the United States and Eastern Canada. Now she dips her gardener's hands in California dirt . . . and reads at Open Mics throughout the San Francisco Bay Area. Her work is stimulated by the contrasts between the wild and the tame in this zone between ocean and hills, a place where cougars may occasionally be seen on the golf course.

Diane is also a watercolorist and collage artist, an experience that both seeds and is seeded by, her poetic imagery. Throughout the spring of 2014, she had a one-woman show of her watercolors at Sofia University in Palo Alto, California.

Please visit Diane Moomey's websites:

> www.dianeleemoomeyart.com
> www.dianeleemoomeywrites.com

www.ingramcontent.com/pod-product-compliance
Lightning Source LLC
Chambersburg PA
CBHW050357280326
41933CB00010BA/1494